Victoria

The Hawthorn Bride

Indigo Dreams Publishing

First Edition: The Hawthorn Bride
First published in Great Britain in 2024 by:
Indigo Dreams Publishing
24, Forest Houses
Cookworthy Moor
Halwill
Beaworthy
Devon
EX21 5UU

www.indigodreamspublishing.com

ISBN 978-1-912876-86-0

British Library Cataloguing in Publication Data. A CIP record for this book can be obtained from the British Library.

Designed and typeset in Palatino Linotype by Indigo Dreams.
Cover design by © Joolz Fleetwood.
Interior illustration by © Finlay Gatehouse.
Printed and bound in Great Britain by 4edge Ltd.

Papers used by Indigo Dreams are recyclable products made from wood grown in sustainable forests following the guidance of the Forest Stewardship Council.

For Finlay and Freya

ACKNOWLEDGEMENTS

Thanks to the editors of the following publications in which some of these poems first appeared: *Acumen, Almanac 2023 (Candlestick Press), After Sylvia* (Nine Arches Press), *Anthropocene, Black Bough Winter Anthology Volume IV, Dream Catcher, Ink Sweat and Tears, Mslexia, Nature and Death Anthology* (Corbel Stone Press), *Pennine Platform, Poetry News, Prole, She is Fierce* (Pan Macmillan), *Spelt, The Emma Press Anthology of Mildly Erotic Verse, The Friday Poem, The Ginkgo Prize Anthology 2022, The Ginko Best Poem of British Landscape Anthology 2022, The Fenland Reed, The Flambard Prizewinners Anthology 2016, The Interpreter's House, The North, The Telegraph, Twenty-One Poems about Wonky Animals* (Candlestick Press), *Under the Radar, Voices for the Silent* (Indigo Dreams), *Wildfire Words Every Breath Anthology 2022.*

'You can Call me Hemlock' was longlisted for the National Poetry Competition, 2024. 'The Hawthorn Bride' won the Candlestick Press Almanac competition, 2023. 'My Dog Brings me Back to Dead Things' was highly commended in the Moth Poetry Prize, 2023. 'Gorse Light' was shortlisted for the Ginkgo Prize Best Poem of UK Landscape, 2022. 'Rainforest in a Shoebox' was highly commended in The Gingko Prize, 2022. 'Pornography for Pandas' and 'I Always Knew I was a Blackthorn' were winners of the Poetry News Members' Competition in 2019 and 2022 respectively. 'The Ivy Crown' was highly commended in the Sylvia Plath Poetry Prize, 2022. 'Heather Honey' was highly commended in the Wildfire Words Every Breath competition, 2022. 'Mast Year' won the Indigo International Wild Nature Poetry Award, 2021. 'Smoking is not Normal Behaviour for Orangutans' came 2nd place in The Lord Whisky Animal Sanctuary Competition 2019. 'Owl Light' won the Otley Poetry Competition, 2018. 'Burning Mouth Syndrome' was runner up in the Mslexia Single Poem competition 2016. 'Little Red' came second place in the Prole Laureate competition 2015.

Heartfelt thanks to Rebecca Goss, Carola Luther and Sally Baker for the insightful editorial advice at various stages of this manuscript. Many poets provided invaluable feedback and support including Sarah Corbett, Dorthe Anderson, Ian Humphreys, Jane Commane, Wendy Pratt, the Nine Lives Poets and the late, great John Foggin.

I am indebted to Gaia Holmes and Ann and Peter Sansom for the inspirational workshops. Also, to Peter Hughes and The Poetry School for the wonderful 'Tree Masterclass.'

Thank you Joolz Fleetwood for the beautiful cover.

Sincere gratitude to Dawn Bauling and Ronnie Goodyer for bringing *The Hawthorn Bride* to life.

Finally, to John and my family for all your love and support.

Also by Victoria Gatehouse

Light After Light (Valley Press, 2018)

The Mechanics of Love (Smith | Doorstop, 2019)

CONTENTS

The Hawthorn Bride

Who'd have thought a blossoming
could carry so much weight, trail
all this slithering light?

The Hawthorn Bride

She's restless and Beltane wild,
veil torn by its circlet of spines.
Who'd have thought a blossoming
could carry so much weight, trail

all this slithering light? Imagine
what it would be to cup her heart –
a yellowhammer in a grotto of thorns.
Savour her scent of musk and decay

a foretaste of what's to come –
the twisted arms of a crone
to hold you through winter's ice.
Don't tell me you wouldn't bleed

for her rioting petals, this cluster of stars
offered up beneath a waxing moon.

Mast Year

In a year that took so much,
the trees gave everything they had.

As you walked solitary paths,
touched by the thin drizzle of spring
conversations were happening between trees;

in the vaults below roots, pale flickers
across vast banks of darkness,
mycorrhizal signalling

a pledge that would bankrupt
for years to come
for this cache of hard mast –

glinting shoals of beech-nuts
cones, open-scaled in your hands,
split gloss of conkers –
what bounty for squirrels, badgers, mice

and you
looking up at a passing jay
an acorn in its beak,
blue-black jewels stitched into its wings.

In dreams you're all
feather, hollowed bone,
throat packed with cupped fruit
as you journey to the scrublands,

heart fit to burst,
every acorn a gift to be wrapped
in the richness of soil

under tangled thickets
of blackthorn, bramble, gorse,
those thorny guardians of saplings.

How it all comes back
to this fierce taproot surge, thousands
of small crowns lifting to the light.

in response to bracken

how it scents the hillside
like medicine and rain
how its ancient symmetry
divides me   leaf-tips melting
to arrowhead   how it closed
off the sky   those Sundays
Dad took us to Otley Chevin
how little time there was
before *coming ready or not*
how I slid the crag   curled
myself to fiddlehead   my heart
the heart of a small animal
each second a brown spore
on a spiralling leaf   steady
tick   tick   of wet foliage
how the dog crashed through
undergrowth   licked the green
light from my skin   pawed up
networks of rhizome
stem after stem   the earth
suddenly electric   wiring itself
with memory   how much I still
want   don't want to be found

Victoria Gatehouse

When My Parents Were Apple Trees

In the summer of my thirteenth year
I made a hammock from old sheets

> knotted between two apple trees
> in the unmown part of the garden.

Both gnarled, one propped at the hip;
together they bore my weight

> as I drowsed through the thick
> secret rustle of hot afternoons

a notebook across my knees
each page a fretwork of shadow and light.

> I scowled away Mum, bearing juice
> and Dad when he checked the knots.

It was to the trees I whispered;
they bent their heads to listen

> as I gently swung, an unripe fruit
> carried like one of their own

green and troubled beneath the skin
a pentagram of pips at the core.

> And when the windfalls came
> my own wasp-sharpness in their flesh

until Mum showed me how to bake them;
just a little sugar, a gentle heat.

Flasher, 1991

it's an hour before dusk & / our mouths
are sweet / we chuck peel into the dappled
shadows of laurels / my eyes are sore / I slip

my lenses out & less / than a metre away
a man / stripping off / I don't realise
he's there until my friend shifts / uneasy

he's watching / blurred against greenery
even without contacts I see / what he
wants / for a couple of seconds it's almost

funny / we shuffle the length of the bench
oranges start to roll / then my friend's yelling
run like fuck & she's up / her feet winged

he's starkers / wreathed in foliage &
panic is making a myth of this / I am
Daphne / sending shoots into tarmac

walls closing hard / around cells / half
way between girl / & tree when my friend
hauls me up by the roots / he is gathering

peel / we don't look back / the policeman
winks / as he asks did we notice what he
wore on his feet / *wasn't looking at his*

- 16 -

feet I say & we all / piss ourselves
my friend & I lose touch / sometimes
I think of her when / skirting that bend

in the lane where laurels / hedge me in
one of the places I've learned to / quicken
how easy it is for rustle / to enter the breath

The Glass Piano

Princess Alexandra of Bavaria suffered from the delusion that she had swallowed a glass piano.

I have turned
myself sideways,
tread thin
in satin slippers,
the small voices
of my petticoats
whispering
don't come close.
My body's a vessel
blown out
from childhood,
that day I swallowed
it whole –
        pedals
depressed
beneath bone,
dampers, strings
turning pins –
all glass.   I fear
marble walls
those who rush past,
the hard snarls
of zinc lions
in the corridors. I will
not ride my horse.
If only someone
would   tune in
to this vast   quietness
piano *piano*
keys pulled
back
from the hammer.

I Always Knew I was a Blackthorn

Not like the other girls,
those Golden Beeches, tripping me up

in the shallows of their roots.
Nothing could grow in their shade.

In the secret thicket of my ribs
I had my knives out

scoring through stories of my childhood,
those *Easy Reading* Ladybird books

where princes lay waste to forests
to rouse her with a delicate kiss.

I was the rod with a barb at its end,
the witch who trapped winter in her bones;

my cold-petal blossoming
lit the frayed edges of solitary lanes.

After the first frosts, a quickening
in the hedgerows, something bitter

grew ripe in the dark, a silver-blue
bloom of fruit, so close to the thorns

and O that first time, there was no prince,
just a Beech Girl, bringing me her gold

her finger on the spindle of my heart,
sloe juice and blood on her lips.

Twenty-One in a Field

Twenty-one has come down in a field –
a pair of party balloons
tight skinned and silvery.

Something must have snagged *two*
into swan-necked collapse
dragging *one* down with it;

a haemorrhage of helium and sparkle.
One, not to be deflated, strains
against the tethers of its other half.

Two is grounded, but twitching
and you're sliding back into twenty-one,
the fields you came down in,

pink-tipped grasses at your fingertips.
How beautiful it was, how much
it hurt, to lie beneath a mirrorball sun

the sky tugging hard on your strings.

Waking Alder

Quiet ache of these hours,
the children at school
a rush of blue notes
from the alder-flute
calling you back to the river.

Here, alongside the cones
of last year's fruit
a tremble of catkins –
the purplish length of the male
the female's delicate scales.

When cut, the alder bleeds as we bleed.

Reach out and trace
this deep spiralling of buds.
Let the alder shore up your banks
breathe a little life
into the waterlogged dreams at your roots.

Forest Bathing in Nutclough Woods

Under this shifting
canopy of oak, birch
sycamore, beech,
a circle of women

fidgety, heads bent
to the dapple-weight
of late spring,
straining to tune in

to root-noise,
hiss of xylem & phloem.
Steady and deep
we'll keep inhaling

phytoncides, as if
somewhere beyond
bark and cambium
the furred rot

of heartwood,
there's a pulse of green
a dryad in each of us
fluorescing.

my life in the verges

up to my neck in cow parsley   so generous
in its shedding of umbels   petal drifts

of aniseed   soft powder my skin as I slip
the day's boundaries   teeter purple

as a spire of rosebay willow herb   pen to page
while my children dream   their faces curled buds

there are woodlice here   unrolling armour
to feast on decay   thistles loosen

themselves to the breeze   bees crawl
dazed   from speckled throats of foxgloves

the grasses spent-up and leggy   a little out
of control   flayed by days of rain & this

is where I find myself   amongst the stragglers
rearranging words   in the small-boned light

here where nettles swarm   & snails make slow
pilgrimage   towards the heart of ferns

My Daughter's Hip Bones

the ache of them   strange fish
   that yawn
inside the bowl of her pelvis
                         It's like
they're grinding against each other

she tells the radiologist   who's gently
explaining how to lie
froggy legs   as if you're swimming

and here she is   my girl
                              surfacing
on a grey screen   the washed-out goggles
of her pubis
the knotted rope of her spine
                         hauled up
      in a drag of bubbles

and I'm imagining what might exist
beneath these lights
                         this fraying gown
the sunken bed of her marrow   sticky
with stem cells
                    distorted starfish reaching
for each other   a mesh of light

on which her bones might grow strong
their language   one I must learn
iliac fossa ramus sacrum

in dreams I'm chanting their bonenames
                         calling them
back
      from dark waters

Hymn for the Ash

After the force of the axe,
the honey bleed,
you must come again;
green-flame tug

curl into heartwood,
limbs sap-sticky, skin
like lichen plaques,
shiver of sugar water

inside phloem. Of late
the wind caries a taint,
a canker in the stalks
of last year's fallen leaves.

Spring brings leaf light
to the woodland floor:
explosions of flowers,
dog violets, garlic

fruit clusters on twigs.
Your own buds fist-tight;
full summer before
your brown-wilt crown

turns to the light, a planet,
half blasted, leaning into its sun.

The Moth

This is her time,
birds dark-stitching telegraph wires

the woods blue shadowed,
crackling with dusk.

The moon untethers her –
she pitches from fence to wall

to leaf, would hurl herself
for miles, such is her faith

and you think of how she gorged
on hawthorn and thyme, spun

herself a mantle, hung tight
inside the blackout

of her own skin
before the breakdown, the forcing

of all that remained
through the veins of her wings

this lit-bulb junkie,
wrecking herself on your porch light.

Pinecone

I write in praise of the female cone
those first tiny buds
spiral bound

on the pedestal of a spring shoot
red-brown scales tilted back –

an invitation
for pollen grains to slip
into the stickiness of ovules.

I write in praise of woody fists
clenched against the rain

of winters fixed in resin glaze
until plates flex apart
in response to warmth

delicate seed-wings, released
to the breeze.

I write in praise of the cone
on my desk –
raised from a needle bed

open to the possibility of wind
even after the seeds have flown.

On Chlorophyll and Haemoglobin

They could be twins
but for a single ion at the heart.

Carbon, hydrogen, nitrogen, oxygen
the building block of life

arranged as porphyrin rings –
how slight   how

vast   the difference
between red and green.

for the Alaskan Wood Frog

because you showed me how cold
can be welcomed into the body like a lover

because your bed is a deep-winter rustle
of leaf litter   because you told me

slow   like the language of the frozen
because you've thinned yourself

to glass   heart quivering on pause
because your brain is a Slush Puppie

your legs brittle enough to snap
because you will not snap

because your veins are steeped
in antifreeze   because you suspend

hope as ice-crystals between the walls
of blood cells   because you never stop

believing in beetles & birdsong   the fat
glisten of peat-bog slugs   because one day

you'll piss out rivers of glucose &
the forest will spring open as you belt out

the old songs in a pond that throbs
with stars   because it's the only way to live

Velvet Shells

*In one of her installations, artist Suze MacMurray lined mussel shells
with velvet.*

They've passed the test,
a tap from Chef's blade,
glimmer of muscle

from those still alive
before the pile-up,
black and blue

on a white plate.
She imagines lovers
scooping out

wine-soaked flesh,
that slow contraction
of spirits in the throat;

on the side, a stack
of coffins, unhinged.
She's a collector

of leftovers
a scavenger
of restaurant bins;

all the way home
that rattle in her hands
and afterwards

hours of scrubbing
the shine back in,
laying them out

with such care
on the kitchen table,
folding crimson velvet

into emptiness,
offering up a prayer
for every little death.

Owl Light

This is the hour she thinks of the field,
unsteady embrace of drystone walls,
feather-tipped grasses, murmuring
their untidy truths, the tooth-hole ruin

of that barn where she first found the pellets –
dark, neat parcels of feathers and fur,
pale curve of bone within, each one
packaged like a gift so she had no choice

but to return every evening, at owl light
and wait for that change in the air, the strike
that comes on silent wings, talons skimming
the tips of the wheat, a half-lifetime ago

and still this bleeding, unseen beneath gold,
the skeletons in her pocket, carried home.

Willow Moon

goddess streaming silver

the river's ancient song

loose curvature of evening

she flows   a dancer

her roots lift tarmac

lads outside the chippy

a shower of golden pollen

dark huddle of terraces

Hecate Helice Belili Circe

a fistful of the old spells

raising the dead

at the car park's edge

drowned by an A road

girls spill from the bars

passers-by chuck empty cans

small-town secrets in her bark

all the swagger of Zeus

on tomorrow's wind

blinds pulled against the moon

gathering slender leaves

love   revenge

The Geese of Sowerby Bridge

You'll see them patrolling the High Street,
ganging up on the corner by *The Long Chimney*,
intimidating passers-by with a show
of downy muscle, a half-lift of wings,

causing tail backs when they choose
to cross the road, a twenty-strong gaggle
impervious to hoots. Always a straggler
who'll pause to shit before reaching the verge.

The *Courier* receives a letter a week
citing *dangerous droppings* and *a town invaded*
and councillors have put up a *Please Do Not Feed*
but there are plenty who bring bread

only to find themselves surrounded,
held hostage by a scrabble of beaks and wings,
the geese strutting bolshie, hissy fitting
on the tarmac like girls fresh from Roxy.

Once I walked the canal path in March,
caught them inching down banks of the Calder,
webbed feet side-stepping takeaway boxes,
Strongbow cans, netting from factory yards,

the females lifting the strong, pale curves
of their necks as they settled on nests
that held fluttering scraps of plastic bags,
the glitter of broken glass.

Indian Blue Peacocks for Sale

Just the sight of a feather in a peacock's tail…makes me sick
~ Charles Darwin, 1860

An advert on sawn-off chipboard
with mobile number and price (sixty-five quid)
and I'd quite like to ring and ask if that's for a chick
or a full-grown bird   and do peacock breeders
(like those who sell puppies) only let them go
to forever homes   and wouldn't that be a farm
or even a country estate because don't peacocks need
space   more than can be found in sunless yards
and aren't their feathers too insistently   luminous
to be trailed over tarmac   displayed against concrete
and how could this small litter-hurling sky
hold their evolution-defying weight
wouldn't plastic cartons splinter their proud beaks
but just supposing   their magnificent throats
didn't gag on the remains of curry sauce and chips
pecked from the astonished mouths of bins
imagine musters of them   dust-bathing in gutters
roosting on the cold shoulders of pylons
acting out their quivering deep-blue rituals
in the reeking alleys of city estates
and how Darwin would have turned away   sickened
at the thought of females holding   the power
to shape future tails   not at all cock-a-hoop
at having to look again   into all those raised eyes

Pornography for Pandas

Yang Guang (Sunshine) raises himself
on hind legs, reaches for the carrot, a little higher

building muscle for the two-minute act to come,
his enclosure dim lit, smooth jazz dreamy

daubed with the urine of Tian Tian (Sweetie)
when last in season - all this to get him in the mood

his bodyweight in food each day for stamina
and now, a forty-inch screen, erected

beyond the bars. His daily viewing –
a male pinning a female's head to the ground

so she can't bite, using his other paw to hoist
her rear end up. A keeper passes, leers

through the bars – *watch and learn, Sunshine.*
Yang Guang shifts the dark smudge of his gaze,

slowly strips down another stalk of bamboo.

Smoking is not Normal Behaviour for Orangutans

says the director of Melaka zoo, as Shirley
a young adult, is put through rehabilitation,

her agile hands, grown proficient
in gathering lit butts from concrete

now reclaiming the textures of banana
and bark, the pliant and the rough

tested against lips, rolled and considered
by teeth and tongue. Nothing here

to draw deep into the burn of her throat,
expel from nostrils in fumy rings

to blasts of laughter, an aiming of screens,
the tossing in of a new flicker

for her to pick up, all of which she's learnt
is normal behaviour for humans.

The Dog who Played With his Shadow

I spot him on the beach, not running
with the other dogs, but bounding back

      and forth, fixated on the moves of
      his darker self, half-moon quiver

of tail, pitch of torso and legs over sand
that bears the slash marks of his claws.

      Abandoned on the moors, his owner says,
      early life unknown, shed and chain at a guess.

Easy to imagine a shiver of wind,
the resulting stutter of light between slats,

      dart of a paw, how he worried
      himself half to death, scratching out

the only game he knew on a concrete floor,
a compulsion that fed, grew vast

      on small offerings of sun and shade.
      And now, this expanse of shingle and sky,

a few seconds of joyous release
before he pins himself back to the ground.

The Principles of Conditioning

Sometimes I think of Pavlov's dogs
Bierka   Murahka   Toi   Ruslan   Beck

      the isolated cages they slept in

the harnesses that restrained them
      the devices   fixed to their necks

Sometimes I think of
steel toecaps   gunning corridors

white-coated researchers   humming
laying out bowlfuls.

Sometimes I think
of bells   buzzers   cold tickings
of a metronome

rates of secretion recorded   precisely
on revolving drums
      bulb-wink-slobber-rush
rising in glass tubes   food

diverted
      from the stomach every time

Sometimes I
think of   saliva
      flooding a starving throat.

           Sometimes
I think of how it felt when he stood behind me

for an ancient oak

knee deep in hedgerows
her leaves have come again
the mother in her   the crone

this small forest of children
for each one   she bled sugar
through mycorrhizal chains

half-dead she   cradles moths
spiders   hornets   ants
owls nest in her powdery lungs

let her stand   until she falls
        cupped brightness
of fox   in soft-bellied trunk

lichen and moss   patching up
the velvet furrows of her ribs
there's sap in her yet

after a night of rain

two snails
on the window

their silvery progress

made in the dark
criss-crossings of desire

I sip my tea

all quiet luminosity
soft as a lip

sealed

Rowan Daughter

the layered silver and bronze
the slim rings around the core
the goddess knelt at my hearth
the prayer whispered into her roots
the toothed leaves within the buds
the uncurled rose of her heart
the light and shade of her blossoming
the charm I carved into the wood
the cut branch a weeping moon
the cross bound in crimson thread
the old spells to keep her from harm
the old spells to keep her from harm

Rainforest in a Shoebox

My girl is dying to show me the emergent layer,
the understory, the canopy, the forest floor.
She has meticulously labelled them all.

Such passion went into their making –
the toilet-roll trunks, the pipe-cleaner branches,
the tissue-twist leaves of emerald and lime,

the buttress roots, luminous with PVU,
the waterfall, a torrent of imagination and shred.
Her box, primary bright, flutters with life –

an orangutan, an ocelot, a two-toed sloth.
Look at the leaf-cuter ants! They have clearly
bitten off more than they can chew.

The teacher has given every child a gold star.
The parents are trying to get to grips
because rainforests can be challenging

not heavy exactly, but awkward
with their flimsy and unpredictable parts
some inadequately glued and dangling.

And we have so many other things to hold.
She knows when a promise is a lie,
my girl, a rainforest pressed to her heart

the lopsided pain of endangered things –
leaf cutter ants, staggering towards extinction
each one with their own shape of load.

Gorse Light

i.m Karen Hall

In the final hours you're unreachable –
plumb the depths of a sleep beyond sleep.

Perhaps you've returned to Embleton Bay
to stride easy across the dunes,
a wild crush of thyme in your wake.
Beyond spiked clumps of marram grass
the beach is a half-moon of uninterrupted gold.

You know you must leave this shore
climb into the ruined shadows
of Dunstanburgh castle, the same faltering
route we took before the hospice,
friends taking turns
to link arms either side, the gorse
out in force. How it blazed for you!

You'll walk it alone, the final mile
across fields, a sky so much bigger
than you could imagine,
prickle of salt on your lips,
coconut sweetness of gorse –

its thorn-lamps burning
all the way to the gate. This time
you'll unlatch it with hands that don't shake
knowing they'll be the curved
arms of a harbour, yellow-horned poppies
to nod gently as you pass,
a bench to watch the tide come in.

My Son Finds a Skull

He lifts it from sand –
how fleshless

the cranial swell,
yellow-creamy

like the top of the milk,
a suggestion of grey

brain-shadow beneath
the surface gloss,

its pin-slim scaffold
of bones, so slight

yet able to hold
the stripped

dark weight of beak.
Look he says, peering

through eye sockets
rinsed by the tide,

both of us imagining
a gull freewheeling the wind.

Phosphorescence

Record this you say and I'm left
in the shallows, holding your phone.

And I capture it all – the moon
low and lush as a forbidden fruit,

you, striking light after light
as you cross the bay; the way

your face, as you turn to wave
is star-varnished like that of a god.

Before you upload, before the flurry
of *likes* for this phenomenon,

there's a moment when your world
is gleaming in my hands. Tonight

I would gulp down this blooming ocean
for a taste of your skin.

Holly King

In the stained-glass dimness
of a midsummer wood

overruled by the heft of oak

he has learnt to sustain
his cravings for berry-fire

on small breakages of light.

In the deep mirrors of his leaves
a reflection of all that is holy.

Come kneel before him

let him teach you
how to live through the dark.

Reservoir Gods

They pay no heed to warning signs
about deep water and toxic blooms
of blue-green algae. These are dangers
which don't concern them, any more
than the fears which make us step
back as they pass, all swagger
in a hit of Hugo Boss. Their F words
lift geese as they take over the path
through ancient pines to a pebbled shore
and the afternoon cracks open, fizzes
like a shaken can, all vigour and foam
as they strip and dive in. They've turned
the air hazy and blue with their splashes,
the bass of their rap, and now, a glint
of muscle as they run, twigs snapping
like bird-bones beneath their feet.
Come winter, they'll hunch into hoodies
test the ice, perhaps, with Christmas Nikes –
but for this summer at least, they know
themselves to be immortal.

Birch | Son

between pale
torsos of birch
the battle cries
of teenage lads
new rulers of
this wild kingdom
phones pocketed
hands free
to build dens
test the give
of rusted bridges
scramble
vine-roped
embankments
of a disused
railway line
birch saplings
always the first
to claim
abandoned
ground
how fast they
shoot up
supple &
lean as whips

Rockpool, you

curator of imagined things
    chalice of saltwater & sky
        O to lift you to my lips & sip

slow   slim fish silvering
    my tongue   to drag
        my net through your fronds

dredge your rock's
    shadowed ledge   that first time
        I came   away with nothing

slender feelers retreated
    not even a bubble of air
        & waiting for your clouds

to settle I knelt
    on a squish of bladder-wrack
        put my faith   in anemone-sway

the languorous
    unfurlings of brittle stars
        no more gazing into the buckets

of others   you hold the strings
    to my mermaid's purse &
        for all the times you offer up

nothing but churn and silt   O my
    bright eye of the tide
        there are days you still   astonish

The Day Comes When I Can't Hear The Crickets

Late August   a walk across moorland
hawthorns shaped by the wind   earth stirred

      to dust by my children's feet
   desire paths through heather
perfume kicked up   startling

the air as they make for the crag
       the valley flushed with a light
            that's almost autumnal.

Listen they say   *listen*
and I'm standing so still   really straining

but it's beyond me now
the frequency of high summer –
      a remembered static in long grasses
lush-verged lanes, trilling –
      a campsite near Whitby

my brother and I   laughing
my mother standing so still
        hair pushed back from her ears

      all those tiny bones inside
      malleus   *incus*   *stapes*

fitting together like my bones
some intricate mechanism   beginning
            to fail

her kids thinking she's having them on
when she tells them she can't hear the crickets.

My Dog Takes me Back to Dead Things

When he doesn't respond to my call
I leave the path, push bracken aside

to find him rolling on badger pelt,
soft-bristle, a cub

not long emerged from the sett
now curled around its own death

mourning bands masking the eyes,
tiny claws like new moons.

And he brings me back to them all:
the savaged, the roadkill, the starved

an instinct that lurks like a wolf
between the base pairs of his DNA.

He must writhe out this obsession
until his coat crawls with decay:

rank stain of fox, wool-scraps
nudged from the carcass of a sheep.

Once there was a starling, half
decomposed on the edge of the road.

I would have walked past, unseeing
but he, addict that he is

nosed deep, nuzzling dark matter
and I came to kneel by the verge

his lead in my hands.
In the spread of that broken bird

a riot of shattered golds;
all I could do to hold him off,

neither of us able
to rub the stars out of its wings.

Burning Mouth Syndrome

The doctor says it's nothing serious, something
she'll just have to live with, a malfunction
of the nerves perhaps, not uncommon in women of her age
and she leaves with a script for a mild antidepressant,
a leaflet counselling moderation in alcohol, tobacco
and spicy foods and when she returns, he says it again
after taking a look at lips, teeth and tongue –
nothing to see and he says it with a smile when she can feel
the bees humming in her blood, the tips of their wings
chafing artery walls and she knows without being told
they're house bees, the ones who feed, clean
and ventilate the hive, pack nectar into the comb
without really tasting it, the ones who wait for mid-life
to take their first orientation flights and she can really
feel the smart of them, the bees in her blood, uncurling
their proboscises to touch the corolla of her heart.
So many years spent licking out hives, all the burn of it
here on her tongue and they're starting to forage now,
to suck sweetness into their honey stomachs, and the doctor
keeps telling her it's nothing as they rise
like stings, the words she's kept in.

Aspen Grove

I dream of them still –
the bone-gleam trees

shivering the banks
of the underworld.

Place an aspen leaf
upon my tongue

and I will speak –

Little Red

So much has been said of me,
the girl in the red velvet cap
with her basket of cake and wine –
so sweet, so kind.

You think I wanted
that do-gooder woodcutter
to snip open the wolf?

It was dark in there,
so magnificently dark
all the better to hear
the surge of his heart
through artery and valve

and I would have stayed
would have raged through his blood
like a blizzard, clawed my fingers
into the pads of his paws

his pelt, a hand-me-down coat
his mouth, my mouth, dripping
from the last kill
not knowing when or how

to stop, only knowing
to stay on that path, collecting stones,
would be the worst kind of death.

Sister, let's speak the language of toads

after the fairytale Diamonds and Toads by Charles Perrault

I was the one who spoke nice
offered the old woman a drink & she
(one of those fairies in disguise)
repaid me in primroses roses sweet-peas
syllables velvety as petals outpourings
of rubies emeralds pearlvomit
the exact moment a prince rode past
one glimpse of my jewel-orchid tongue
& he was on his knees

six years of marriage my prince
smug & rich from diamond-streams
their tumbling facets each one
a wound in my throat & how he loves
to force the flowerheads out of me
chrysanthemum chrysanthemum
peony peony florets overblown
& taking my breath I just can't
swallow them anymore

my foul-mouth sister let's summon
what's festered under leaf-litter for years
the fire-bellied the helmeted the spadefoot
I want to feel them crawl up my gullet
tongue the shape of them in my cheek
luscious with slime warty-backed Sister
let's burrow into venomous & glandular
together we'll break the choked surfaces
of ponds spawn wild & riotous strings
.

You Can Call Me Hemlock

For too long I've been masquerading
as cow parsley, all elegant pretence

these hairless stems, lace-edged leaves,
teeny umbrella flowerings.

Ditch the expectation of aniseed –
my odour is a stoning of mouse.

Close up, I'm mottled as winter thighs,
purple & blousy with alkaloids.

I can be   difficult. I have it in me
to make witches fly. Did you know

I was the death of Socrates,
how he trembled, his pupils

blown out to dark moons?
I love it when you call me names –

Wormlicks, Beaver Poison, Stinkweed.
Think of me as the toxic celery

in your wild-carrot bouquet.
Strip my stalk to a whistle &

I'll hollow you out with my tune.

Conversation with the Mole

He speaks of subterranean churches,
the sacred hush of tunnelled ground

confesses it's all about the worms,
their luscious-pink squirm in the throat.

Sometimes he hoards them in chambers
half-alive – to come back to later.
I admit I have poems like that.

My shoulders thicken,
a blunt, shovel-strength in my hands
as we swim beneath the earth

throwing up mountains

to dismantle and remake the dark,
root-scented corridors
in which insects hunker down;

startle of moth-wing
of grub-shine, the coal-seam
backs of beetles, unfastening

a glint of the language
I thought I'd lost.

I confess it's all about the words,
the way they hum larval on the tongue.

Darwin's Daughter and the Stinkhorns

Here, where light is thinnest,
a clutch of moon-eggs, breaking
out of their skins
to surge into being
each olive-grey tip, shameless,
& writhing with blowflies.

This could be a fairy-tale –
your basket & cloak,
the path between oaks, except
you're a hunter, a nose for
that base note of *phallus impuvidus*
wafting from deadwood & fern.

You raise a sharpened stick
and strike. What a stink
you've raised, a raft
of fruiting bodies at your feet,
this pale ooze of flesh
you'll burn in a locked room.

All to save the maids
their swoons, mushrooms too lewd
for what your father would call
the *inferior female mind*
but even he can't explain
the survival of the most obscene.

You don't tell him about the dreams
where you're winged,
drawn by their carrion reek
to gorge, spore-sticky & just think
how far you could carry them,
the places they might rise.

Hazel Divination

every morning she walks
the forest's loamy path

above her the dense

& shifting drapery
of summer's end

slim drippings of green

as she dowses for words
with a forked hazel rod

silversnakes coiled in roots

deepening glint of salmon
in the bowl of a sacred well

sudden quiver of wood

here in a nutshell
the line-ending she needs

The Ivy Crown

remember   many autumns ago
Dionysus came to squat in the ruined barn

you found him   in the corner of a September dusk
a roosting of bats in his cloak   remember

his dark-berry eyes   warm nectar on his lips
how you swarmed his walls   tender rootlets cast out

remember   how he bound   and unbound you
wove you a slim ivy crown   how you corkscrewed

dead trunks   maenad-wild   wasp-drunk
the acid-green flowers which covered your skin

remember the gloss he laid over your stones   how
the last of the insects came to crawl in your veins

how your leaves turned   from juvenile lobes
to feral hearts   remember how he made you live

how you cut yourself free   to live

Devil's Spit Day

There's a patch of garden
you left for the brambles to claim.

How quickly they anchored
suckering roots and what froths
of blossom, before the sweet lobes

you pinched off, fat and lush,
your fingertips, lips, glossed up
on purple until September's end.

Now decay has crawled under your fence,
trees losing their grip, bleeding gold,
tendrils of rot in the stone

of the fruit and you know he's out there
in steel-toe-capped boots, pissing
through hoops for the hell of it, spitting

juice like blood, holding you on the edge
of his dark, feckless tongue.

.

Heather Honey

those nights   a cough wracked you from sleep
to shudder in a blanket   the back door ajar

you couldn't get enough   of the thin cold air
a sting on every breath   those nights you unscrewed

the honey a friend left in the porch   deep twist
of the spoon   unsettling   pockets of air in the gel

the hot-water melt of it   glazing your throat
a wood-smoke tang   you couldn't taste   those nights

you turned bee   rose from the hive   to face
the purple chill of the moors   those crawling hours

endless bell-shaped flowers   how gently you extended
your proboscis   lifted the grain from each heart

as slow fever licked the roots   somehow you flew above it
your blood all thick amber-shine   those nights the heather

brought you back   to the steadying hum of your breath

Turnout

Unexpected, this white-knuckle lawn,
leather-capped clusters
beneath the trees, tender gills
surfacing from deadwood

roly-poly bodies sponging
off the rain. It's the thought
of what they might be that holds you
in your dressing gown, still

on a damp October lunchtime –
saffron milkcups, chanterelles,
destroying angels, slippery jacks.
Theirs, a poetry that fruits

on decay, slides through the lips
on a promise of raw meat
or silk. You'll savour it slow
this bellyful of possibility and rot.

My Son and the Spiders

He lifts them from the futile
slopes of bath and sink
his hands almost
the hands of a man

not always

I remember mock-screams
in the playground
clover-mites thumbed
to flecks of blood

a teen lifting wings from a moth
broken glimmer
of scales in the air

and don't let's forget how
rain brings out the monsters
snails welly-stomped
to a shining
mosaic of pain

the small lives our children
have deadened
how quickly they learn

all the power he has in his hands
almost the hands of a man

and now this spider
gentled
in the shallows of his palm

Walking Through the Churchyard with my Daughter

We kick up the grass, all swish
in this place of slumped stones,

their language blurred by lichen
lost to centuries of weather.

Someone has been here before us
on a ride-on mower, or just passing

through in hoodie with strimmer –
clearing a path for the living,

thick-quilting the beds of the dead.
The rowans are loaded with berries,

another summer almost done.
Her hand slips from mine

as she runs ahead to Street Dance
at the church hall. Even the dead

must stir at this scent -
the long, green cut of the air.

Learning to Walk in Your Boots
For Karen

Plenty of wear in them you said,
the woods all green tenderness,

both of us knowing your walking days
were coming to an end. I never

told you they were half a size too small,
to wear them would involve

a not insignificant pinch of the toes.
Now the trees have given up

their ghosts to the wind, only
the beeches hold on, defiantly bronze,

tiny creatures wintering
in the twists of their leaves.

Some days the small paths are enough:
slipways between drystone walls.

I remember our last walk, how you
stumbled into the jewel-glow of moss,

your ground unstable. Relentless
those tendrils of tumour in your brain.

That belly laugh of yours if I told you
I'm learning to live with the nip

seams starting to give,
to take on the contours of my feet.

Your boots are moving like they used to;
easy over streams, the frozen roots

of beeches, already slim-budded,
still clinging to last year's leaves.

The Man who Grows Marigolds in Urinals

His farm hunches beneath the rim
of the moors, thickset to withstand
the Pennine winds, which rattle
the bones of antique ploughs
lurking like dinosaurs in his yard
alongside cartwheels and Belfast sinks,
the disconnected and unplumbed things

like this row of urinals fixed to the wall
where marigolds bloom on old seams of piss,
bowls flushed with pleated light. He nips
out the dead and they just keep coming
right through to October's end –
Halloween, All Souls, Día de los Muertos –
small lanterns to guide our ghosts home.

Planting a Hedgerow at Clough Head Farm

As the year darkens, teeters on the edge
of breaking, I think back to a blustery
Sunday in May, how my son took

a mattock to stony ground as I
heeled in hawthorn, dog-rose, hazel.
How we anchored supports, swigged tea

from tin mugs, the valley laid out
before us, reservoir-bright,
fields bristling with thistles and docks

every leaf-bud an unlit fuse,
my daughter crouched by the gate
as rescue sheep fed from her palms.

How I promised the pipistrelles
would come, the dormice, the hedgehogs,
the toads, and quiet on my breath

a prayer - for thrushes to settle
between thorns and sing fierce joy,
lunar moths to find safe passage

on the harshest of nights and *please*
small lives will scuttle green corridors
long after the kids have left home.

reed bed

the steel in November skies, the wind a blade, the heron an ancient

god, the scythe a new moon in your hands, the tethered strength

of the roots that shored the banks, the long cry of the wind

in the stems, the great lengths I ran through my fingers

the close weave of the thatch, the green scent

of our bed, the salt hollow at your throat

the bound pipe of staggered reeds

the wild flood of notes, deep

song of the river

on your

lips

Elder Mother

Approach her with care.
Boundaries will dissolve and reform as you enter her realm.
Lay a silver coin at the base of her trunk.
You're here to honour the thirteenth moon.
In May you packed your wounds with the sting of new growth.
On Midsummer's Eve, her flowerings, their wine-lovely spin
& the Elf King beckoning from the haze of the otherworld.
You very nearly followed.
Come Samhain, her leaf-bones, risen to skitter on the wind.
Now her fruit's black and blue, ravaged by starling, by thrush.
Uncloaked, she reveals her true wizened self,
she who knows what it means to be hunted as witch.
See the buds she keeps in reserve, their knotted gleam.
Some days it's enough just to breathe.
Your shadow has crossed into hers.
Offer a strand of hair, the half-moon
clippings from your nails.
Before you take a sliver of her bark, a pact –
sealed with your blood, her sap.
To give back your own wood when you become tree.

Yew Needle

There are days you dream
of beginning all over again
like this churchyard yew:
ancient scales of its bark
softly flaking away, the smooth
spiralled into the rough.

There are days you could lay
new rings around an outgrown heart,
leave all this fossilised silence
to the spiders and moths.

You dream of supple branches
returning to the crackle of earth
to root trunks all over again.
Time to slip this choker of aril beads,
take up a green and dangerous needle
and stitch yourself a new skin.

NOTES

A number of these poems are a personal response to the trees and shrubs of the Ogham – hawthorn, apple, blackthorn, alder, ash, pine, willow, oak, rowan, gorse, holly, birch, aspen, hazel, ivy, heather, bramble, reed, alder and yew.

Page 16: Flasher – In Greek mythology, the nymph Daphne turns into a laurel after being pursued by Apollo.

Page 19: I Always Knew I was a Blackthorn – Blackthorn has long been associated with dark magic. Its impenetrable thickets are thought to have inspired the forest of thorns in the fairy tale Sleeping Beauty.

Page 21: Waking Alder – When cut, alder wood turns red.

Page 22: Forest Bathing in Nutclough Woods – Phytoncides are antibacterial and antifungal plant compounds, believed to have health benefits when inhaled.

Page 28: On Chlorophyll and Haemoglobin – Chlorophyll and haemoglobin are very similar in structure. Haemoglobin has an atom of iron at the centre, chlorophyll has magnesium.

Page 29: for the Alaskan Wood Frog – These frogs survive winter by flooding their cells with glucose which acts as an antifreeze. They remain frozen for months with no heartbeat/breath until spring when they thaw out and loose the excess glucose through the urine.

Page 35: Indian Blue Peacocks for Sale – Darwin disliked peacocks because they didn't fit with his theory of evolution. Eventually (and reluctantly) he came up with the 'sexual selection' theory – that females chose the most extravagantly plumaged males as partners.

Page 36: Pornography for Pandas – Panda 'sex' recordings are sometimes shown to captive pandas to encourage them to mate.

Page 42: Rowan Daughter – In accordance with folklore, rowan crosses, bound in red thread, were made for protection.

Page 55: Aspen Grove – In mythology, placing an aspen leaf under the tongue bestows the gift of eloquence.

Page 57: Sister, let's speak the language of toads – In the fairytale by Charles Perrault, the 'nice' sister is charmed to speak in flowers and jewels. Her 'difficult' sister is cursed to speak in toads.

Page 60: Darwin's Daughter and the Stinkhorns: *"Armed with a pointed stick, in hunting cloak and gloves, she would sniff her way through the wood to fall upon her victim and poke his putrid carcass into her basket. She burnt them in deepest secrecy on the drawing room fire, because of the morals of the maids."* ~ Gwen Ravert on Etty Darwin, Period Piece (1952).

Page 61: Hazel Divination – Forked branches of hazel were, and still are, used for dowsing. In ancient folklore, hazels grew around a sacred pool, dropping nuts into the water to be eaten by salmon, a fish revered by Druids. The nuts themselves were associated with poetic inspiration.

Page 62: The Ivy Crown – In Greek mythology, Dionysus, god of wine, fertility and ecstasy, used ivy to ensnare women who refused to worship him. Bound to him in ritual madness, they became the maenads, literally translated as the 'raving ones.'

Page 63: Devil's Spit Day – On 'Devils' Spit Day' in late September, the devil allegedly fell to earth, landing in a blackberry bush and deliberately ruining the fruit.

Page 73: Elder Mother – In folklore, elder trees were home to the Elder Mother or witch. Cutting the wood could incur her wrath. At mid-summer, the elder was believed to be a portal to the faerie realm.

Indigo Dreams Publishing Ltd
24, Forest Houses
Cookworthy Moor
Halwill
Beaworthy
Devon
EX21 5UU
www.indigodreamspublishing.com